FROM HOLE TO WHOLE

ONE WHO KNOWS ONESELF KNOWS THE WORLD

Himani Chandna

ISBN
Paperback 979-8-89475-312-6
Hardcase 979-8-89544-509-9

Contents

Preface

This book is a collection of insights that I had on my journey to discover my true authentic self. It started out as me journaling in my small diary all that I was experiencing and practicing in my daily life to find out "Who am I, really?." As I was treading this path and going more inwards, I realized that all that I had been doing in my life so far unconsciously has always been in some way or the other to prove a point outside and to satisfy the false ego. I started realizing that true success is not just about material wealth and external validations but more about inner peace and a sense of fulfilment. This realization ignited an inner transformation in me and the more I connected with myself through meditation and by being in a state of witness consciousness the more I started getting these insights on how to live a more meaningful and fulfilling life with a sense of purpose.

I knocked on many doors and many places in my sincere quest to find out what really is the truth only to realize that the answers are always within. No doubt each of those doors played a signification role in breaking the external shell of my conditioned consciousness and in putting me a step forward in this journey. But ultimately, only to make me realize that there is nowhere to go but within. This book is my account of experiences that take a deep dive into recognizing your true nature, empowering yourself by mastering your mind and living a life of purpose by focusing on inner growth, by living in the present moment and by finding out what you are truly meant to do.

Acknowledgements

It is never possible in any shape or form to ever thank your parents. This is the first place perhaps where a soul experiences what unconditional love could feel like and I cannot thank my parents enough for nurturing me like how nature would nurture its creation with utmost deep love, care and total freedom.

My deepest gratitude and heartfelt thanks to my mother and father, and to my lovely sisters Sonal and Charu for giving me an environment throughout my life of unconditional love, unwavering support and total encouragement to pursue a life of my dreams, to pursue a life of love and purpose.

Nov 6th, 2022

Bengaluru, India

1. Nature of the Mind

It is the mind that runs the show of your life. Most of us take actions from the thoughts that originate from the mind. Thoughts lead to actions. Actions lead to Karma (the concept of 'action' or 'deed' that sets in the motion of cause and effect). Karma leaves traces as *Samskaras*[1] (stimulus–response) *like water leaves traces after it is dried up.* Samskara is carried on to the next life and that is how we keep on coming and going into the cycle of birth and death. Mind is full of impressions from this lifetime and many other lifetimes. Most of our actions and reactions are because of our past experiences and samskaras (tendencies).

The moment we realize we are just souls in a second we feel so free. Free from the ever-oscillating mind. When you realize you are just an energy and nothing more, it immediately frees you from the clutches of the mind. But this can happen only with an experience may be. But

---

[1] *Samskaras - Samskaras are mental impressions, recollections or psychological imprints. In Hindu philosophies, samskaras are a basis for the development of karma theory.*

an intellectual understanding is the first step perhaps. Remind yourself in every second that you are a soul, you are an energy that has taken a body only for the sole purpose of freeing itself. Practice this daily and grace will flow automatically in your life. The only purpose of your birth is to merge back with the supreme soul. Be cautious of building any karma with anyone. Because of our five senses we keep on building karma because of our likes and dislikes, our cravings and aversions. Real freedom is when you are free from all of it.

Surrender all your karmas to the Higher Self or the Divine. Be free from the results of all your actions. Be light, be natural. Work on improving your intuition so that you perform only those actions that are guided by your soul and not by your mind. Soul has to guide the mind to do the actions and not the other way round. Strengthen your soul so much that only actions guided by the soul are performed and the only way to strengthen your soul is by quietening your mind. Mind can be silenced by Meditation and Sevā. Sevā is the selfless service of doing good to others.

Sevā is always selfless or else it cannot be called Sevā. By observing your mind, you can silence your mind. By listening to your soul always you slowly and gradually start becoming a master of yourself. Always listen to what your soul guides you to be because this is how you truly become powerful. No money, no fame nothing in the world out there can ever make you powerful. You become your own master by always listening to what your soul guides you to do.

Your mind can consider it to be illogical or logical does not really matter just do it. Whatever your soul guides you to do. Every step every second connect with your soul to guide you, to talk to you, to show you the path. Do not rest till you can access the absolute truth. Words only come from the mind. Silence has no language. Always be an observer of your emotions erupting, feelings and thoughts arising. When you come to a witness state everything outside of you will start appearing like a dream, something that you are not a part of but simply witnessing it from the outside.

The biggest fight is always between the mind and the intuition. The mind has become so powerful that the voice of soul has almost become silent. Mind is *Saṃsāra (world)*. Intuition is your soul's wisdom. When you get an intuition like a sudden clash of thunder that is the message from your soul. Some call it as higher-self; some call it as true-self. Mind is fiction and fiction is not reality. Absolute reality is where the fiction of your mind does not exist. Just meditate and access the wisdom of your soul because your soul dwells in absolute reality and it never goes wrong. Truth always touches the one who lives truthfully.

Even if you are sitting at a religious place, it could be that your soul is guiding you to be somewhere else. But since our minds are conditioned to copy and follow, we continue sitting there as everyone else is doing the same and because the mind has been conditioned to believe it is the right thing to do. However, in the path of self-mastery you have to invoke the master within you, the guru-tattva within you. You need to invoke that inner voice guiding you what must be done in that moment. And that guidance is neither right or wrong it simply is. Right and wrong are the dualities of the mind. The voice of the soul is free from any duality. Nonduality is about how we live 'here and now' without choosing one thing against other.

There is no spiritual place though there are many religious places. You can visit thousand and one religious places but you will not be able to have a single glimpse of spirituality. Spirituality is an inward journey whereas religion is an outward pursuit. You may taste silence at religious places but that will not remain with you for long. To be rooted in silence permanently - there is nowhere to go, but in.

Something that really helps in the path of self-mastery is solitude. Being just by yourself for a long period of time gives you an opportunity to witness your emotions at all times. When it becomes a constant habit to witness your emotions or feelings you slowly start becoming free from it. There is an awareness that dawns in you that actually no emotions or feelings no matter how good or how bad have the ability to shake you. And like this slowly and slowly you start becoming centered. And this centeredness is priceless, is golden and the only way to achieve this state is by becoming a witness.

No person, place or situation has an effect on your true-self. It has an effect on your "I," "Ego" only. There have been so many times that we have felt different emotions sometimes positive and sometimes negative even when the external situation or the person has remained the same. This clearly shows that happiness and sorrow all are within us. We can only bring out that which is already present within us. To remain centered is to remain witness to all that erupts from within us.

When you practice being a witness to everything happening within you slowly and slowly you would start becoming more and more powerful and you will start glowing with an inner shine. Only a person who is full of self-love can only truly love someone outside. Practicing self-love means understanding your needs completely and believing that you are worthy of them. The more you love yourself and give yourself what you need the less you will demand it from others.

The more you are in self-love the more you gain the ability to love anyone and everyone unconditionally. One of the aspects of self-love is to always listen to your inner voice, your soul's voice, your intuition. The reigns of your life should be given to your soul and not to your mind. When your soul is on the driving seat it will drive you straight back to your real home. The home that you have totally and completely forgotten as the mind has taken you millions of miles away from it with no way back.

I felt guided to listen to this Gurbani Shabad today "Bandhae Khoj Dhil Har Roj Naa Fir Paraesaanee Maahi."2 It simply means that there is nowhere to go but within. All things are available within you and not with someone else or somewhere outside. No matter how strong, appealing or powerful the external situation or person is always listen to your inner voice. This is the only way to make direct connection with your soul. It is the only true connection that you truly need to sail through anything thrown at you in this worldly materialistic life.

Always have full faith in your inner power, your inner strength because you are part of the divine so you are divine yourself. A drop of ocean water is ocean itself. Write your own Geeta, your own Bible. Each soul has its own path, its own journey so never compare yourself or your journey with others and that is how you become a true and original being. Observe all emotions that come out of you when you encounter a particular situation or a person. Simply become a witness of it and you will observe that slowly and slowly the emotions are fading away. Practice this to realize this phenomenon.

---

2 This Gurbani Shabad is extracted from Sri Guru Granth Sahib meaning 'O human being, search your own heart every day, and do not wander around in confusion.

March 11th, 2023
Bengaluru, India

2. Rewiring the Brain

So why is meditation necessary? Not all people understand this. Some people say that why bother, we are healthy, there is no problem in our life, why should we meditate. Some people might also say that even though thoughts run too much but then what is the problem in life. I am doing fine, so why is it important to meditate and reduce thoughts?

This is just like a caterpillar saying, "What is the need to become a butterfly." You must have read how an egg becomes a caterpillar and how the caterpillar metamorphizes into a butterfly. A caterpillar which walks on the ground turns itself into a cocoon and creates a kind of cover around itself. The body of the caterpillar changes inside the cocoon and a transformation takes place inside it. After some time, its wings start emerging out of the cocoon. These wings break the outside cover and ultimately the butterfly starts flying. In a similar manner, nature has designed us humans in such a way that it has made only half and has left the other half on us. It is your choice if you want to fly or not and if you do then you will have to become a butterfly. This design of ours is so that we can ultimately find true happiness and it is not possible without this transformation.

One must change the brain for this metamorphism. Why do so many unnecessary thoughts come? This is because we have not rewired our brain. There are about 86 billion cells in the brain. Scientists say that out of these 16 billion cells are there in the frontal cortex-the front part of the brain which thinks. So, thoughts are bound to come. Now it is up to us how do we reduce that expense because a lot of our energy, perhaps more than 96% of our energy is wasted in useless thinking.

Meditation is not to be understood as mere praying, or submitting to some scriptural or human authority, participating in rituals, religious paraphernalia, wearing religious robes, going for pilgrimages etc. Also, it is not a silent or loud mechanical repetition of some mantra, phrase, word etc. Such robotic repetitions can only dull the mind. Instead, true meditation is living a practical daily life with contemplation on who we truly are. Living your day-to-day life with compassion, gratitude and surrender in order to facilitate a conscious inner transformation.

An interesting spiritual fact is that there is a sixth sense in every human being which resides in absolute reality-pure awareness. This sixth sense is activated when we meditate. Mind cannot be silent. Mind is chaos. Mind is traffic. Mind is sequence of thoughts. Like walking is when you move your legs. Mind is when you jump from one thought to other - A to B, B to C, C to D, D to C etc. Silence and mind are diametrically opposites. This is where meditation can help you in controlling the stream of thoughts.

Sit in a comfortable posture, close your eyes and watch your breath inclusive of all the other sounds happening around you. If you witness only the breath then it would be focusing or concentration and that would be opposite of meditation. This will work perfectly if you witness your breath inclusive of all other sounds and body sensations.

Start as short as 5 minutes in the morning. Then 5 minutes in the morning and 5 minutes in the evening. When you become comfortable with 5 minutes then increase it by 5 minutes after every 15 days. Maximum 30 minutes of meditation daily will bring a change in your life. This would certainly help in controlling the mind.

And when the juice of meditation starts coming, then you start understanding the fact that now you have started living, you feel the power and the strength within you and you start becoming more creative. Meditation will melt and change your samskaras-tendencies-impressions that you have been carrying since lifetimes. Remember you are the ancestor who will create the blueprint for your future generations.

3. Become an Observer

Have we ever observed our bodies closely, the contractions that we feel in our stomach, palpitations in the heart, the heart beating faster because of particular thoughts or emotions or feelings or in the presence of some people. Why do these sensations manifest in the body. And when the situation is gone, the person is gone, those feelings and emotions are gone then those sensations in the body are gone too. If you closely observe what is happening in your body then you automatically become free from it. Whatever you observe or experience in a witness mode simply has no power over you. You are not entangled with it. Whatever you become aware of you become free from it. Being aware is the first step towards anything. It is only when we get entangled in a situation, with a person or in an emotion that we become a slave of it. Living an authentic life is being free from all sorts of slavery. When you live an authentic life, you are calm. When you do not live an authentic life there is a certain fear always lingering inside of you and that gets revealed on your face.

Being in the witness mode is a continuous practice. You have to remind yourself again and again to come back to the witness mode. When we are fully blossomed in our true-self which is love, peace and joy then we can never hurt anyone or be negative. It is only when we operate from a place of lack that we knowingly or unknowingly hurt others. Again, and again try to do all those things which bring you in high vibration. Again, and again remind yourself to not to spend your energy in anything that brings you in low vibration. Real power, real courage lies in the fact that you can recognize and become aware of any situation which is in low vibration and immediately take steps to come out of it into a space of high vibration.

High vibration is the place of love, peace and joy and low vibration is the place of hate, negativity and worry. You are the universe. You have infinite power within you. Do not become a slave of any low vibrational person, place or situation. It is fear and comfort that stop us from coming out of any low vibrational situation. We fear of what will happen next or worry if the step that I am taking to come out of my present situation will it lead to a better situation or result or not.

Life is new every moment. We should try new things all the time or else we would start setting ourselves in some mold. Do not become any mold. You can do anything and everything. Do only and only those things, those conversations, those jobs, those travels, those relationships, those friendships, those connections that take you into high vibration. Every moment life is to be lived peacefully and joyfully. If that is not happening then you are not on the right track. When life gives you challenges and obstacles the choice is always in your hand to become bitter or better.

Do not be a rebel without a cause but instead be courageous and fearless. Fear drains and exhausts our life force, our energy and stops us from coming into high vibration. The tendency of the human mind is to copy, to avoid the unknown, to comprehend the unknown. But the path of spiritual journey is the opposite - it requires you to clear up everything that you know from others. Because spiritual awakening is the state of pure consciousness - a mirror free of dust. Do not listen to the stories, do not presume, do not extrapolate; this is your journey, so listen to your heart and go by your experience.

The most important criteria that you must consider when choosing anything in life is how you feel about it. Energy is the true barometer of deciding what you should do or should not do. If it brings you in high vibration, then it is the truth coming from your higher self. Everything that exists in this cosmos is energy and that is the ultimate truth. Whatever brings you in high vibration is the truth for you and you must not ignore it at any cost. If it does not bring you in high vibration then you can easily reject it. It is not meant for you.

No need to copy others just do whatever brings you in high vibration where you feel peaceful and joyful. You are the consciousness yourself. Love yourself, respect yourself, forgive yourself, hug yourself. It is very important to sit in some moments of silence every day. It is only when the mind is in a relaxed or in a calm state will the real stuff emerge on the top. Mind has been conditioned by your upbringing, your culture, your society and everything around you.

All that you know is borrowed from your family, society and religion. All conditioning and ideologies belong to the mind and mind is created by what you know as crowd. Your mind is crowd. You are some of your mother and some of your father, some of your brother or sister and some of your friends. You are multiplication of all that you consider as truth. You are a crowd. Your truth is not truth, your self is not true self. It is just an accumulation of knowledge and conditioning.

Put the soul in the driving seat and not the mind. Be fearless in your pursuit without the baggage of past failures or societal judgements. Always remember mind is the false ego-self given by the family/society/religion and people around you. But there is a possibility of transcending this false ego-self and that is when you will come to know that you are the limitless infinity like the universe. Like a wave comes to know it is the ocean. When cloud comes to know it is the sky. When your false ego-self is not there then you realise you are everything. You are eternal.

Whenever you are in a stressful situation start taking long deep breaths, focus on your breath and come into witness mode. Start observing the current stressful situation as a third person, detached from it completely. One thing we all must do in our lives is to spend some time alone daily with ourselves. When you start enjoying your own company and do not feel lonely it automatically makes you very powerful, courageous and fearless. You are no more dependent on any joy from anyone or anything outside and this is a very empowering state.

Loneliness is a result of duality of mind and awakening is transcendence of mind. Aloneness does not equate to loneliness. Loneliness is ugly. Aloneness is our reality. Aloneness is when you find yourself complete without others. When you need not worry about who is there and who is not, when your joy comes from within.

Ego buildup happens when you consider yourself to be higher than others but when you are empowered you do not consider yourself to be high or low. You simply are natural and joyful with everyone and everything around you. When you are empowered, you are not trying to prove anything to anyone. You are not looking for validation or appreciation from outside.

Ego and self-respect are diametrical opposites poles. Ego belongs to the outer realm and self-respect belongs to the inner world. Ego trip is a matter of mind and self-respect is a matter of soul. Ego is based on doubts, whereas self-respect is based on trust. Ego is a state of aggression or depression and self-respect is a state of transformation. Ego is a prison; self-respect is freedom.

The nature of the mind is to always be in activity. That is why sometimes when you have nothing to do you start becoming restless. You start doubting and questioning yourself if you are not doing enough or if you are not good enough. That is why it is important to meditate so that mind comes to rest in a natural way. Mind becomes relaxed automatically through meditation. As a result of this, you are filled with more energy to do things and most importantly you get the energy to do the soul guided things.

Love yourself enough so that you do not look for validations or compliments from outside. Remind yourself of all the good qualities and attributes that you have. Comparing yourself to others is a sure shot way of depleting your energy and bringing yourself down into low vibration. Alarm yourself immediately the moment you notice you are doing that. Do not be too hard on yourself. It is ok there could be days you do not feel like doing anything.

Take it easy on yourself. Relax and rejuvenate but at no time derate or degrade yourself or doubt and judge yourself. You are the light that should shine bright wherever it goes. People should feel uplifted in your presence and even if some do not it does not matter. You always do your own thing and love and appreciate yourself at all times.

Listen to your heart more than your mind. Do all those things where you feel a sensation or something expanding in your heart and what brings a genuine and fulfilling smile on your face. People pleasing behavior automatically takes you down into low vibration. Your soul is crushed inside but from the outside you are artificially trying to please someone. All these habits and tendencies over a long period of time make you a slave of external situations and people. The biggest and truest joy is in finding your true-self, is in being your true-self. It is very important to prioritize yourself over the wants of others from you. Do not act to please.

March 14th, 2023
Bengaluru, India

4. Breaking Behavioural Patterns

There are many times when a particular person especially the one that we love does not react or respond the way we expect them to be, or when a situation does not turn out to be the way we expected it to be. Then in that case we tend to get into a habit of hurting ourselves like not doing the things we normally enjoyed doing, not going out, not dressing up, loss of appetite, loss of energy, loss of interest in mundane things. All these habits immediately take us away from our center, from our true-self and bring us down into low vibration.

The moment you start observing this behavior, this pattern in you, it is time to break it. Immediately alarm yourself and do all those things which will rise you up in high vibration. Again, and again give those reminders to yourself. Again, and again alarm yourself and bounce back into high vibration. By repeatedly doing all those things which bring you back in high vibration will break this cycle, this pattern, this tendency of staying in low vibration whenever things or people do not go as per your expectations.

What we do again and again always becomes a habit. So, make sure doing high vibrational things becomes your habit. What will bring you into a state of high vibration is a very individualistic thing. There is no rule book for it. What is high vibrational for one person might not be the case for the other and vice-versa. So become aware of your own self and reflect and identify what brings you into high vibration.

It could be anything, literally anything in this world right from travelling to new places, to writing, to dancing, to singing, to painting, to running, to cooking, to dressing up to the nines, to sitting quietly in your own presence, to meditating etc. Always do what comes naturally from within. Whatever is natural is always the truth for you. Staying in your own truth empowers you like nothing else can ever will.

March 22nd, 2023

Bengaluru, India

5. Authentic Power

There are only two kinds of power. Authentic internal power and external power. External power describes the things outside of us that we desire and make us feel like we are somebody or have something to give us value. It is the cars we drive, the titles we carry, the money we make, the perfect spouse and the perfect handbag and the perfect outfit and whatever that makes you feel good because it is an external thing. You can tell if these things have a hold on you because when they are taken away a painful void is left behind if they have a hold on you.

Authentic internal power really is the only power that matters. It simply means that you are strong from within. You do not need any external association or validation to feel powerful. Once you start getting that internal authentic power or let us say a state of authentic empowerment you start living more consciously on a more enlightened path because that is what you are looking for in life – authentic power. Authentic empowerment comes from the inside. It means aligning your personality with your soul.

When you feel powerful you might want to showcase it to others but when you are empowered there is a zero need for a show-off. You are simply basking in your glory. You are shining from within and that is what reflects on the outside too. There is no need or urge to prove your strength or power to others. When you are empowered, you simply let things flow naturally through you. You become very natural when you are empowered. This is because there is a sense of fulfillment from within. You are not operating from a place of lack.

Only when we operate from a place of lack that we become desperate and try to fill it with something or the other without even realizing if it is coming naturally to us or not. And this is how we enter into relationships which turn out to be toxic and co-dependent, do jobs that are not even true to our nature or abilities but are fancied by the world, fabricate a powerful image in front of others only to fill up and hide the lack within.

March 23rd, 2023

Bengaluru, India

6. Living in the Present Moment

Recognizing what depletes and drains your energy is the first step towards self-care and self-love. Buddha had rightly said that desires are the root cause of your misery. Most of the times when our desire is not fulfilled or something that we have been waiting for long does not materialize then notice there is something that happens inside your body. You might feel your heart beating faster or might feel knots in your stomach etc. This is how our body reacts to stressful situations. It is very easy to lose track of your ultimate path when things do not go your way.

You might feel like giving up all because of the sadness. But real courage is in walking the path all along no matter what. The best rest in times of distress is to go deep into silence and to take proper sleep. Deep rest heals both the body and the mind. Silence and deep sleep both will help in bringing the mind to rest. Deep sleep is the dreamless sleep where mind takes actual rest. Otherwise, normal sleeping is almost like being awake only since in such a sleep mind is fully functional in the form of dreams.

Being in the present moment is the only reality. Difficult situations, difficult challenges would come in your life again and again no matter how old or experienced you are. But the one who can overcome it each time is the real winner. All we have to do in this life is to recognize our patterns and break them. Sometimes some people and relationships come in your life to break you, to shake you but ultimately to make you.

So many hidden talents and abilities which were lying dormant in you come to the surface because of the presence of these people, of such connections. They teach you so much directly or indirectly. Recognize it and send your blessings to these people every day. It is perhaps only because of them or such experiences that you started walking on the path to upgrade yourself.

March 25th, 2023

Bengaluru, India

7. Listening to Your Intuition

Removing all your attachments to external dependencies is the ultimate sign of freedom. Love that is infested with co-dependency and toxic attachments will make you hollow just like termites do to the wood. It is very important to again and again alert yourself and make yourself conscious if any of your relationships or connections is leading towards making you a parasite sucking energy from others for its survival and fulfillment. If you do not exist then nothing in this world exists for you.

So, it is very important to take care of yourself first. If you are in good shape physically, mentally and emotionally then the reality that you create for yourself will simply reflect it. It is very important to differentiate between the voice of your soul and the voice of your mind. The soul will never guide you wrong. It comes with utmost clarity with no iota of doubt.

Listening to your self - your soul is a continuous process. It cannot be learned in a day. One of the ways to reduce the chattering of the mind is to get into Sevā.

Every individual is capable of acting in such a way that he or she can benefit the entire community and make a difference to other lives. Big or small whatever it is spend your time in doing some Sevā. This would help in taking the attention off from your chattering mind. Self has no questions no doubts. It is the mind only which creates all the noise. All the panic.

The more your mind is quietened the more your self would come in the driving seat. When the self is in the driving seat it will always drive your straight. The answer to any of your questions or doubts does not exist outside. The answer always comes from within. The more you will go outside to seek answers the more you will deplete the power of your inner voice. Remember, life is not a problem to be solved but a mystery to be lived.

One of the ways or rather the only way to empower your self is to take actions and decisions on your own. The more you will do that the more you will strengthen the self. The more you will go outside like seeking help from astrology, tarot reading, psychics, clairvoyants etc. the weaker your self will become.

It might happen that things and situations will pull you down but again and again rise up till you ultimately realize your true self. You cannot live an empowered and fulfilled life based on someone else's mind or intuition. Act as per your own gut instinct, what is that your heart is telling you to do. If there is ever a question of choosing between the heart and the mind, choose heart because the heart is always right. Mind is a creation of the society. It has been educated. Mind has been given to you by the society, not by the existence. The heart is unpolluted, it is pure existence.

March 27th, 2023

Bengaluru, India

8. Attachments

Sometimes you must change your place to clear your energy. If you are feeling stuck for too long then it is time to make a shift. A shift that is guided by your self and not by your mind. Sit in meditation and calm the ripples of thoughts taking birth in your mind. Recognize the patterns and the wounds that you need to heal. The patterns that are making you feel stuck.

One sign of toxic attachments and relationship wounds is always looking for validation and love from the other person. You feel loved, appreciated and validated only when that particular person loves you. When you have a wound like this you are always in chasing mode. You are always craving for love from that person whom you have very conveniently kept on a pedestal as the ultimate source of your happiness and fulfillment.

When others do not give you love or attention it is fine but when this particular person does not give you the love and attention that you are craving for then it is starts affecting you very badly. With a toxic relationship wound like this you start losing interest in things that you used to enjoy earlier. You even start losing interest in life. You enjoy only when they are around. There is a lack of excitement, thrill and happiness in their absence. You feel as if only their love can make you alive and happy again. Recognize if you have this pattern. Recognize if you find it difficult to move on or let go of the person who is not reciprocating your love. Recognizing and accepting the problem is the first step in solving any problem.

To break this pattern, divert all your love and attention to the divine. Talk to the divine or the higher self, pray to it to give you the strength and inner guidance in breaking this pattern once and for all and setting you free from all desires and attachments. Take a break and spend some time alone. Talk to people who are in high vibration in this phase. Totally disconnect on the physical level from your object of affection. Then slowly try to disconnect at a mental level. But physical disconnect is the first important step you must take or else your energy will be fully drained leaving you all exhausted with no energy to move on and do other things.

Simply witness if their thoughts come. Good or bad thoughts whatever it may be simply observe them and let them go away on their own. Do not associate yourself with these thoughts. Take long hot water showers. Pamper yourself in whichever way you like but do that. Engage in some Sevā activity as it utilizes your energy in a more constructive manner and helps in grounding you. Selfless

Sevā purifies you and this journey is all about breaking your patterns and mental conditionings.

Gratitude, pure love and freedom come only when you learn to let go. Love is a journey to wholeness and letting go is the key. Love is as delicate as a butterfly; you catch it and it dies. Do not try to possess another person. Freedom should be the basis of love otherwise it is bound to fail. Love and meditation are the state of "letting go" and they bring you closer to your true Self.

9. Giving is a Blessing

Whenever you are suffering because of a heartbreak or your desires not getting fulfilled, simply take the attention away from your wants and start helping others in whichever way possible. The more you will focus on helping others the lesser the impact of your own worries will become. If someone is not choosing you then it is better you choose yourself and instead of moaning your time away start helping others. When we help others, it brings us back in high vibration.

Whatever you feel is a lack in your life start giving that same thing to others. If you feel there is lack of love in your life start giving love to others. If you feel people do not appreciate you enough start appreciating others. Sometimes when we face a lot of rejection in our lives then we tend to build boundaries and walls around us. We become very guarded, doubtful and insecure. Best way to bring those walls down is to hug others. Hug yourself, your parents, your family, your friends, strangers that you meet. Hugging others in a loving way has a lot of healing effect on our mind and body as well. Only those can ever give who truly have in them.

The stressful energy that gets pent up is released harmoniously and not in some disastrous violent manner. Start giving more and more and it will help you in coming out of your small mind and the sorrow and misery built up within. Try writing down your experiences. It is a very good way of relaxing and healing yourself. Do not type them instead write them with a pen and paper. As you write each word you release that energy into the universe.

Never compare yourself with others. Just go deep within and explore what is that you are good at, something that you can do exceptionally well than somebody else. It is not like nature has not endowed you with uniqueness, everybody is unique and everybody has many talents. The existence never discriminates. Existence loves you as much as others. So, no need to complain, no need to compare, just find what is that you are good at and grow with that.

March 29th, 2023

Bengaluru, India

10. Depression and its Antidote

There could be times when you would feel everything is meaningless, that you are simply moving in circles with no destination or goals. But remember this is just a phase and is not something permanent. Just get into silence, talk less, cut yourself off for some time and simply witness this phase. Let it pass naturally. Focus on your breath, witness your thoughts, your emotions and mediate more. Take more rest and deep sleep. Mind might give you a million reasons not to do any of it. Immediately alarm yourself when this is happening. Silence really helps in overcoming a lot of stressful situations.

Maximum health issues arise from anger, resentment and negativity. Anything that makes you feel stuck should be abandoned. Anger, regret, guilt, break-ups, failures, painful memories, future worries should be overcome or else they simply drain your energy. If energy is not freed, then one cannot rise above and you remain stuck forever.

Some ways to overcome feelings of depression, anxiety etc. are listening to music that uplifts you, dancing naturally and freely along with it, doing vigorous physical activity. Going for long walks preferably in nature just by yourself. Drinking lots of water as it instantly relaxes and calms your mind. Also, by surprising your own self from time to time by doing things that you have never done before. Always remember there is a crack in everything that's how life gets in.

March 30ᵗʰ, 2023

Bengaluru, India

11. The Purpose of Solitude

Solitude is the best gift that you can ever give yourself. It is only when you are totally by yourself are you able to observe many things about your innate behavior, your patterns, your emotions, your thoughts way closely than ever before. Some of the deepest enquiries like "Who Am I" occur in silence, in solitude. You start paying attention to small details for e.g. the dream you had the previous night. Why did that dream come. Why am I able to remember dreams sometimes and sometimes I totally forget them. What is a dream? Who watches the dream? Who remembers it?

Your observations become very deep in life. You start questioning the fundamental aspects of existence, of life itself. It gives you an opportunity to listen to wisdom or talks of other people who are also on the path of discovering themselves, who are on the path of self-mastery or who are already enlightened (self-realized).

Why do I feel strong attachments and love towards one person and not the other. Why my emotions or opinions change from time to time for people or situations/events. What is this phenomenon? Who Am I? Why sometimes I ask these questions and sometimes not?

There are two problems that every human being suffers from and those are the possessiveness towards objects and attachments with people. These are the two points that keep you confused and clouded. If you can become aware that you possess nothing and stop identifying with possessions and achievements and relate with people but do not get attached to them then you too can get self-realized.

Get into hermit mode again and again to quieten your restless mind and do not give in to any external stimulant. The ultimate freedom is when you have no attachments, no desires, no cravings, no aversions, just total pure bliss.

Since thoughts and emotions are ever changing there is no point in associating with them or holding on to them. Seek that never changes. Nothing external should shake your inner bliss and peace. That is the state everyone should strive to achieve. There could be many ways to achieve this state and this is where comes the importance of listening to your higher self. You can call it supreme soul, universe, awareness, consciousness, cosmic intelligence, divine, god whatever name you want to give to it.

You must find the truth on your own. No one can give it to you. You need to have a seeking approach rather than a questioning approach to realize the Self. Adi Shankaracharya (an enlightened master) said "Brahman - Satyam Jagat - Mithyā" but you must make it your own truth. You must realize it on your own.

Many times, you might feel stifled and suffocated while walking on this path. It would feel like you are dying a physical death. It would feel as if nothing is making sense be it external or internal but remember this is just a phase. And like every other phase this will get over soon too. It becomes very important to stay one pointed and focused on this path no matter what is happening outside. Make sure that you stay connected with the people who are also on this journey so that time and again you can get some healing from them as required.

This is because you might feel like sharing your challenges and experiences during this phase but it can be understood only by the people who are walking on the same path. Share your experiences, your journey only with those who are on the same wavelength, same vibrational frequency as yours. With others whatever you share could simply be noise or humbug. You do not have to explain yourself or prove yourself to anyone. Get rid of this habit. It only brings your energy down and puts you in self-doubt.

Best way to live is to live moment by moment. Sometimes that moment can be happy and sometimes not so happy, so what simply keep on flowing. It makes life so light and burden-free way if you live it moment by moment. No need to apply the mind just live by the moment. The happier and content you start becoming the more happiness you will start spreading. We can only give what we have. Isn't it?

Life is the abundance that you feel when you do good to others, when you create something, when you meditate. It is the connection that you feel with the existence. Whatever the circumstances if you can live in the present moment in such a way that you feel the connection with the infinite vastness inside of you is what probably life is all about. Your happiness and contentment are in your own hands. No one can give it to you and no one can take it away from you. Sing when you feel like, dance when you feel like, write when you feel like, do nothing at all when you feel like. Just be happy in every moment. Happiness is a practice.

It is very important to become completely aware of conversations that take you away from your Self and drag you too much into the matters of the worldly mind. If such conversations are draining your energy, then become aware and alarmed instantly to put a stop to it else you would be dragged into it with full force.

You need to know where to put a stop in anything that you do. And this can happen only when you are alert and conscious to recognize the fact that you are moving away from your center.

There is no bigger master in this world than your own life and its experiences. Observe and watch it carefully and consciously and learn from it. Life itself will teach you more than any person or text could ever do. Try to learn from your own experiences as it is the best teacher and the lesson stays firm in you forever. Live and embrace life completely and in its totality with full acceptance and effortless surrender. And you will be amazed to see how alive you will become as a result.

Confidence is about 'moving inward' and ego is about 'moving outward'. Confidence is to move to your center and ego is to move away from your center. Ego says, "I shall show you - Who am I?" Confidence says, "I know myself - Let the world know." Ego is an altered inflated or deflated state of your identity. Confidence is knowing your true self. When you move inward you reach the center of your being.

You are the center point, the focal point of your life. Treat and respect yourself like that. When you extract your joy, your happiness, your fulfillment from outside then you will always be left empty handed as the source of extraction is external and you have no control over anything that is external. But when you become the source of giving joy, happiness and fulfillment to others then you are always full and abundant as the source is internal and infinite. You will never be left empty handed when you become a giver. Because giving itself fills you up.

We have always thought that when we give, we are losing but in fact it is just the opposite. When we give, we gain. You can only give when you are feeling abundant and are full of gratitude. Only when you believe that you have more than enough can you ever get empowered to truly give. What a joy it is in giving.

When you become a giver, you become the divine because giving is an innate quality of the divine. Find out the different ways in which you can give to others. It could be just about anything but inculcate this habit of giving in your life. Giving brings you in a state of high vibration and pure love immediately. It helps in breaking the barrier of your Ego, I, Me, Mine. Like nature simply gives you also just give without expecting anything in return.

March 31ˢᵗ, 2023

Bengaluru, India

12. Abiding in the Self

One of the important factors that you would need to be very aware of on your path to discovering your true Self is the kind of company that you keep. If you surround yourself with the people who are also on the path of self-mastery then the journey becomes a tad bit easy because they are walking and talking the same language as you are.

On the contrary if you are surrounded by people who only operate from the limited conditioned mind then it is like having a lot of potholes in your journey. They can drain you a lot and tend to pull you towards their conditioned mindset and the unconscious materialistic ways of living. They can make your hardwiring that you are consciously trying to get rid of even tighter. That is why there is this need of solitude, some time alone just by yourself till you are firmly established in the Self and cannot be shaken anymore.

Every day is a brand-new day on this journey and you discover something new about yourself every single day. That is the beauty of walking on this path. There could be days that you are so low that you start doubting your own intentions to find your true Self. You feel sad, angry and hopeless. But then again comes a brand-new day with a lot of hope and freshness and courage to keep on walking. Universe will send you a lot of signals to keep your spirit high and hope alive. It fills you with a lot of positivity. So never give up just because you encounter some low days. Remember if you have set your intention right and are putting your attention to it then it will definitely happen.

In this journey travelling, exploring new places also opens a lot of things in you. You can get a lot of insights when you travel to new locations. Your energy also changes when you travel. You have not come down to the "earth school" to settle so never become stagnant anywhere. Your higher self might guide you to go to a new place. Do not ignore this voice. Your patterns, hardwiring of the mind also gets broken when you travel to new locations.

It is important that you take enough deep sleep and rest so that you do not feel drained to do any high vibrational activity. Unconsciously spending endless hours on the internet and social media simply clutters your brain. Take periods of technology detox from time to time. You lose your ability to think creatively and innovatively when you spend so much time with technology and social media.

Staying indoors in four closed walls all the time stifles your inner growth. Make sure wherever you stay has enough sunlight, air and nature coming in. Remember we are the nature so when we lose connection with nature, we lose connection with ourselves. Consciously make that decision to stay at a place where there is a lot of nature around. In case you do not have this option then try to bring some nature inside your home by placing small pots of indoor plants or natural flowers wherever possible.

We destroy the innocence of children by imposing and projecting our desires on them. Life springs out of freedom and not just by giving birth to a child. Life simply happens - No one should plan for it especially your life should not be planned by others. The worst thing that one can do to others is to force them to do anything that does not come naturally to them. True sign of loving someone is setting them free. So just let others be the way they want to be. Do not judge. And never lose your child like innocence in the process, its precious and very rare. An intellectual person with innocence is a spiritual person. Intellect without innocence is cunningness and cleverness can only strengthen the mind. A spiritual person is more of a heart than of a mind.

April 7th, 2023

Bengaluru, India

13. Life is Here and Now

Life is to be lived in the moment. If you get an instinct to do something, just go ahead and do it. When you do not pay attention to your instincts or your inner voice then slowly and gradually it becomes low and diffused and once again the patterns of the mind win or take over. The only way to break the shackles of the mind is to act on your instincts. This way over a period of time you will cultivate the habit of listening to your instincts and you will start dissolving the patterns and the boundaries of the mind. What a free life this would be. Amazing! Thinking about it itself increases the life force in you.

There is no one like you who has ever been born before or would be born after. Treasure your existence. It is so precious and unique. Just be natural the way you are and that is how your originality will flow in the existence. The only person you need to know is you, the only person you need to understand is you. Once you know yourself you will know the entire world. What you experience with your five senses is just a fragment of things. Just a fragment of reality. What a waste human life would be if you miss the chance of knowing your true self. What a waste human life would be just trying to be like others, trying to follow others, doing what others do, getting what others get.

Life of total slavery. All human beings are salves of something or the other till they achieve the ultimate freedom of knowing who they truly are. Rest all is a life of slavery. Mostly people who tread on the path of self-mastery have a streak of rebel in them right from their childhood. They would always question the status quo or do things that are considered risky or away from the usual societal or cultural norms. They might be considered stubborn, arrogant or egotistical as well because of such capabilities.

Your awakening is a divine phenomenon. Your quest to find your true Self must be very sincere and unshakeable. Killing your inner voice and bowing down to the noise of the mind just to please people or external situations/events is like doing a suicide. The journey to freedom is not a one-day thing. It is a continuous journey of uncovering your layers, uncovering your masks one by one. Every time you uncover a major layer of yourself the mind would tempt you to consider it as the destination, as your true Self. But there is more and more to unmask till you reach your ultimate self.

It could happen during your unmasking process that at a particular juncture you might think that now I have found my soul purpose or my soul mission and you might start working on it as well. And this soul purpose - soul mission could be anything teaching yoga, healing others, becoming a meditation teacher, opening an NGO, making videos on social media platforms to educate others etc. And you might think this is it. This is what I have been born for.

But this is not the end, always remember there could be many more things and different things that you might do at a later stage as you unmask yourself more and more. It is a journey not a destination. Do not stop and settle anywhere. The unmasking will then continue to happen on it is own naturally. Remember you are always guided by your higher self on this path. So, keep on walking with faith and surrender. The right people and the right opportunities will come your way to help you and guide you to unmask yourself more and more.

April 13th, 2023
Bengaluru, India

14. Letting Go

In your journey to self-mastery a lot of times you will get triggered especially by your near and dear ones, family members, friends, colleagues etc. The triggers mostly come from the people close to you because you hold the maximum karma of your lifetime/s with these people. Most of your shadow side comes on the surface through these triggers. So do not get bogged down by these triggers. These triggers allow you to heal your deep-set wounds that you have been carrying from your past lifetimes and this lifetime too. These triggers allow you to break your patterns. If you are never triggered you would never heal because your issues would never come on the surface.

Do not get shaken up by these triggers. Simply watch and observe what is that you need to heal, what is the pattern that you need to break. Make a note of them and then create an action plan around them. Triggers and healing process are a part and parcel of this journey towards your higher self. You would lose connections with a lot of people in this journey once their purpose in your life is over. You will keep on getting the same lesson, same kind of people or situations/events in your life till you learn them completely, till you heal the wound completely.

Once the lesson is learnt, that person or situation/event never gets repeated and you take one step higher in your journey towards ascension, towards enlightenment, towards the ultimate freedom. Many words for the same thing. These words would only be understood by the people who are on this journey of self-realization. For others, all of this could simply be an imagination or hallucination since they are not in that level of awareness.

Laziness is a major roadblock on this path. It can delay your ascension considerably. Consciously become aware whenever you are becoming lazy and act upon it. But at the same time do not get too hard on yourself. Remember loving yourself is the key mantra! There could be days when you might feel as if you are a living corpse doing all the mundane things around you like a robot, as if your mind and body are dead and everything is happening mechanically. But this is just a phase, a part of the journey. So many patterns of your ego, of your conditioning, of your preconceived beliefs and notions are getting broken in this process and it would make you question your whole existence.

Because all that you had known till now or had considered as the reality is getting broken, getting shattered. Whenever a pattern is broken or ego is shed it creates a lot of negativity initially because the mind and the ego want to hold on to the old. Layer after layer of what your mind, your ego had believed to be true is getting peeled off. It is bound to make your mind and ego sad and restless. That is why you might feel so dead in your body and mind for days together.

It is like how a cocoon sheds its layers to become a caterpillar and the caterpillar sheds its layers to become the butterfly. This entire process requires multiple layers to be shed. Layer after layer as you go deeper you are approaching death - the death of the ego. It is bound to be painful and scary. And without death how can you be reborn? If you are ready to let go then the death of the ego will happen and you will be resurrected and born again. What the caterpillar calls the end of the world, the soul calls the butterfly.

It could take one lifetime or birth after birth to shed these layers of mind, of ego to become the ever-pure Self. Overall, this is a journey towards coming closer to your soul and letting that shine in various aspects of life. This can turn you into a more confident, expressive and ultimately, happier person as you align more closely with your "true self."

April 16ᵗʰ, 2023

Bengaluru, India

15. Strength of Spiritual Practices

The journey towards the self is all about breaking your patterns, healing your inner child wounds and resolving your deep-set traumas. As a result of this, it is very important to tap into your sub-conscious mind to find the root cause of your issues. Why do you feel stifled and suffocated? Why do you feel stuck with certain emotional patterns such as toxic attachment issues or co-dependent behaviors?

One of the sub-conscious healing sessions for a young woman revealed that when she was born, she was an unwanted child born in the hope of a boy. Also, as a young girl of 13-14 years she felt the lack of physical touch and physical expression of love in her life. And she carried these inner child wounds for many years. The warmth of a caring physical touch was experienced only when there was an achievement or a worldly success.

A warm physical touch and a loving hug should be given unconditionally simply as an expression of pure love that you feel for the other person. It becomes very important for parents to give loving warm hugs to their children so that they experience an outer expression of their parent's unconditional love right from a very young age. This way they will not look for validation outside and will not build trauma bonds with others.

This could seem like a very small thing but it has a huge impact on children. That woman's inner child was wounded for so many years that is why she deeply longed for love outside from people who were not even capable of providing it. And this is happening everywhere, where in the absence of love only unhealthy attachments get formed and wherever there is an attachment misery always follows. Self-love, self-care and the true meaning of it should be taught at a very young age so that we build strong, loving and fulfilled human beings. When this is not done the patterns of lack of self-love, forming unhealthy attachments are carried forward generation after generation.

The physical hug is not an expression of attachment or any emotion but that of pure love that you already are. Only someone who has become love can give love to others. Rest all expressions are simply superficial outer paraphernalia infested with attachment. Anything that is done out of attachment would always seek something in return sooner or later. Simply a business transaction. Anything that is love simply flows.

Start giving hugs full of love to your parents, siblings, children, friends, strangers, anyone and everyone. Love heals. Hugs heal. When there is lack of self-love or when one has inner child wounds then people build walls around them. They become very guarded. That is when they stop giving love and in return the flow of love back into in their life also stops. Your true nature is love and the purpose of this human birth of yours is to get back to your true nature.

Spiritual practices such as yoga, breath work like pranayama, meditation, listening to knowledge, doing Sevā are of utmost importance in keeping your mind peaceful and calm. The practice of yoga immerses us into the present moment. To know that right now is all there is. If we can just connect to the present moment we enter into a space of timelessness where we are not necessarily trying to get somewhere, we are not necessarily trying to acquire something and that ultimately brings a sense of peace and fulfillment because that is all we have is this moment right here, right now. All the great philosophers have talked about this, all the great teachers have talked about this. However, when you practice yoga, you can have the experience on your own versus thinking of it as just a concept.

You can listen to your higher self only when your mind is calm and quiet. No matter how busy or lazy you are maintaining a discipline of doing your spiritual practices daily is of great significance. This would help tremendously in your journey back to your core. Be your own GPS. Be your own guiding light. But this light can only shine when the mind is silent. Do not fall into any trap of the outer world which takes you away from your spiritual practices. This would only delay your journey and nothing else.

No matter how tempting the external situation/event or person is always put knowledge and spiritual practices at the fore front. Stay away from people who are too caught up in materialism and have completely forgotten that they are just souls visiting planet earth to grow and transcend. Talking and explaining your journey to such people is simply banging your head against the wall. At least at the beginning share your journey, your experiences only with those who are at your level of awareness until you are fully rooted and fully blossomed in your true self. You are the light it will shine no matter what.

April 22ⁿᵈ, 2023

Bengaluru, India

16. Boredom is a Blessing

The crux of this journey is based on pain. Pain is an inevitable part of this journey of realizing your true self. Mainly because whatever you had considered normal till now is not normal anymore. You start feeling like a complete outsider to everything around you. You do not feel like doing things that you normally used to do. You are losing relationships, losing jobs basically everything around which you had built your so-called world. The falsehood is breaking and the truth has started taking birth.

And birth is a painful process. You might feel so dark, so hopeless, so lifeless for days but do not ever give up. It is simply a birthing process of the truth. The outer layers of your mind are shedding and the truth is revealing itself layer after layer. You will be surprised to see that the higher self or the divine never lets you fall in this journey. There surely might be low days but the power of the self will always make you rise. People might judge you since you are no longer behaving like them and they might start considering you as impractical or eccentric too.

But remember they are not on this journey of waking up from deep slumber. The sleeping ones can never know the truth. And the one who is awakened definitely knows he is not sleeping. Always and always be cautious of the company that you keep. It should be of the ones who are awake or are sincerely wanting to wake up.

This is important until you are fully blossomed to spread your fragrance to the whole humanity. It is like how a gardener (higher self here) protects a bud till it is fully blossomed into a flower. We are born original but the pattern of the collective mind of the world has made us into copies of each other. That is why it is called a rat race because everyone is like a rat. No matter who wins you still remain a rat. You are born to be enlightened do not let anyone or anything stop you from being who you truly are.

It is the path of the brave ones, courageous ones. It is not for the faint hearted. It could happen many times in your journey that your self has guided you to do something but doing that something breaks the patterns of the mind, the ego or your societal conditionings. So, in order to save itself, the mind would make that situation highly comfortable for you. But remember it is a trap to keep you stuck in your comfort zone. Because growth always happens out of the comfort zone.

For e.g. your self has guided you to leave your present job and take up something new. Your situation in your present job would suddenly become too good for you,

you will start getting all the appreciations out of nowhere. Simply because mind/maya/ego does not want your higher self to win. It does not want your inner voice to win. At this point if you do not listen to your inner guidance-the voice of the higher self then you dis-empower it. And this continuous dis-empowerment of the inner voice that we have been doing birth after birth has made the voice of the soul so feeble and so silent for almost all of the humanity.

The more you listen to your inner voice the more empowered and louder it becomes. And slowly and slowly with practice the places would get reversed. The self would be in the driving seat and the mind would be in the passenger seat. And when the higher-self drives you, it will always make you reach the destination.

Only when you are bored of the mundane things of life that your quest for truth gets ignited. Becoming bored is a blessing. Most of the people never get bored of the worldly life. They eat, sleep, run after achievements, chase titles and labels and they think that is it, that is all. This is what life is all about. It is like being a frog in the well who has never been out of the well and thinks that the well is the beginning and the end of life. A very sorry state of human birth. A precious human life simply wasted in being inside the well only.

You need to possess a true warrior spirit to step outside of this well and walk towards your higher self. Even if one person in this whole world feels that spark inside and gets ignited to start their journey towards knowing who they truly are then I believe the purpose of this book getting written is solved.

The enemies that the "warrior" self has to fight in this journey of self-mastery are attachments, false ego-mind, anger, lust, jealousy, greed, comparison, competition and many more. All these enemies would be placed on your path time and again till you completely destroy them. You will be tested again and again so never give up even if you fail multiple times. If your quest to know your true self has sincerely been ignited then be rest assured that liberation is not too far. Always remember, a diamond is a piece of coal that never gave up.

17. Dropping Self-Doubt

This journey is of unmasking and un-layering. Many times, it might happen that after many layers of your conditioned mind are shed, you would feel this is it, you have arrived but you will be surprised to realize that there is a lot more to shed off, a lot more of the dirt to be removed because a lot more is getting stored in your sub-conscious mind daily.

Self-doubt is a poison in this path. Remember self will never guide you wrong. And the only way to listen to the voice of your self is by quieting the mind. Give your meditation, yoga and Sevā the highest priority in your life. Rest all will come and go and change like seasons do but only the "never changing self" will take you back home, to the divine.

The universe, the multi-verse is infinite. You are only a speck of dust in it and your mind knows very little of this infinite awareness that encompasses you. Keeping an open mind is an essential aspect towards discovering anything in life be it outside of you or inside of you. Self is infinite and ever knowing. With your limited mind you can never understand it fully. Just because you do not know does not mean it does not exist.

So, it is best to still the mind, to quieten the mind for the self to shine through itself. Attachment is a big deterrent on this path and letting go of anything or anybody gives you the greatest strength. You are most empowered when you have the ability to let go. The more you attach yourself to a person, a place or a situation/event the more you create stubborn impressions - samskara's in your mind. And these samskara's drive your life and your life choices. As a result, you are never able to come out of the chakravyuh-maze-trap of the world.

Seeing oneness in everything is the default nature of the enlightened one. They do not have to make an effort. It simply is their nature, their being. Try to practice oneness in your daily routine, daily life. Not taking anything personally and simply accepting it as coming from the higher self - divine. Try to differentiate less and less amongst people, places and events. Take everything as one self or divine experiencing itself through everything that exists. This will be an effort in the beginning since it is just an intellectual understanding at this stage.

But this will definitely fast track your own journey of becoming that oneness, of being that oneness. Training your mind to inculcate such habits really helps. You have to train your mind like a young child. Every single time you ignore your inner voice, you weaken it, you do not feed it. And every single time you listen to your inner guidance, you feed it, you empower it.

What you can experience in silence can never be experienced in words. Go for silence retreats from time to time to connect with your true self, to develop the habit of listening to your inner voice. The only purpose of human birth is to become your true authentic self and do whatever it guides you to do which is sometimes referred as soul purpose or soul mission. You just need to become hollow and empty like a flute so that divine can play his music through you. You simply are an instrument of the divine and realizing and becoming that is your only purpose. There is nothing else, nothing else and nothing else to be done.

All what you are doing right now are simply acts out of total ignorance. All activities of your life be it good or bad in the worldly terms that take you away from your true authentic self is a worthless act and keeps you bound in the cycle of birth and death. The acts that you do which are guided by your true self is your true dharma. The acts that you do which are guided by your ego-mid is karma.

Dharma has no credit or debit. It leaves no impressions. And karma is what you have to give and take as result of which you are born again and again into this worldly cycle. Do not build more karma as you only have to repay it, just do your dharma - acts guided by the true self.

Your mind will play a lot of tricks on this path. Be very cautious of it. Whenever you get a thought or an emotion simply witness it first. Do not react. Only respond. All thoughts and emotions will wither away in some time just like clouds do in the sky. Get out of the habit of giving justifications and seeking validations. They really disempower the soul.

Follow your spiritual practices such as mediation etc. incessantly to make the journey less arduous. Focus on your breath whenever your mind is going haywire. Breathing slowly and deeply helps us in becoming centered. Focusing on the breath helps in becoming calm. Focusing on the breath silences, quietens the mind. Long and relaxed deep breaths calm the nervous system. Close your eyes, take long deep breaths and simply focus on the breath.

Mind and breath have a deep connection. To confirm this, one can conduct a simple experiment on oneself. For example, watch your breathing pattern when you are frightened, or when you are engaged in sensuous activity, or when you are angry. To see the difference, compare it with the breathing pattern when you are calm and at peace. In both events, the rhythm of the breath would be different.

Walking, taking long walks plays an important role too. Long walks close to the nature not in the hustle bustle of traffic and not amidst concrete walls. Food also sometimes plays an important role in this journey of becoming the best version of yourself. If your digestion is not proper it gets very difficult to sit in meditation or do your spiritual practices such as yoga, pranayama etc.

Digestion problems can cause severe headaches which cripples you in doing anything. It is very important that you focus on keeping your body fit and healthy so that you can engage in high vibrational activities and sit in meditation. Just imagine how you feel when you are sick - so tired and exhausted to do anything.

No matter what your eating habits are right now be it vegetarian or non -vegetarian start your meditation. As the energy of your meditation will increase so will increase the intelligence of your body and the body itself will demand what is right for it and what is not. There is no need to add any moral values to this but to simply start meditating and experience it for your own.

As you progress on this spiritual journey you will realize that it is the path of compassion and the very idea to kill is disturbing. You will realize that the life that is running inside you is also running inside the chicken you have just killed to satisfy your taste buds. Eating simple fresh sattvic vegetarian food in moderate quantities keeps your prana (life force) high and keeps laziness at bay.

Stay away from any form of intoxication. This journey is all about facing life with full alertness rather than escaping it. Your consciousness is already burdened so much with anxieties, worries, anguish, that you take a drink and feel good in the moment because your consciousness goes to sleep and you get a temporary escape from facing the reality. But remember it is only temporary.

Another form of intoxication is when people run to monasteries and ashrams to escape life whenever it hits them hard but even there they remain in the same turmoil. The problem is the limited understanding of life. And understanding and balance in life comes from living life in all its dimensions. Life is bitter and sweet, laughter and tears. One who does not know how to cry, cannot know how to laugh. Do not choose one thing against the other. Life is not a dirty pond; life is a river flowing to the sea. Life is not just a seed; life is a tree. Live life in its totality. Embrace everything life has to offer you.

Watch through the problems. 80% of the problems are imaginary and 10% you cannot do anything about. 10% are real and work through them. Do the needful. You will always find the solution inside of yourself. Just watch.

April 28th, 2023

Bengaluru, India

18. Infinite Patience

One of the key milestones in this journey of self-mastery is patience. The biggest lesson you learn on this path is to be patient and not just patience but a joyful patience. Learn to wait. One who waits is given the highest. Timelines are only created by the mind to keep you bound. You can attain the highest in an instant or not even after multiple births.

Keep on walking and never look back. Never look back to the past experiences, past emotions, past feelings, past events. When you do not look back you simply do not look back at anything. Your mind will try to remind you of your past mistakes, past experiences, people, events be it anything good or a not so good past. Immediately get alarmed by this trick of the mind which is trying to drag you down. Never read the book of your life backwards.

Mind is chaos, mind is noise because the mind is 'doing'. Meditation (dhyana) is non-doing. You cannot stop your mind. But you can transcend your mind altogether. Be a witness, let the thoughts come and go. Do not identify, do not cooperate, do not resist. By and by thoughts will become powerless.

Start observing, witnessing such thoughts. They will go away quickly the moment you start observing them. When you get into the habit of observing your thoughts, emotions, feelings like a witness/ third party then they have no control over you, then you can never get entangled in them. Mind's memory of the past and worries of the future is the biggest obstacle set by the mind to keep you entangled.

Our worries of the future are due to fear of pain and desire for sensory pleasures. One who is free from past-memory and future-anticipation, he is quite happy within, under all circumstances. Being in the present moment always is real freedom. Only when you are entangled by the mind you react. When you are not entangled by the mind you respond. The more you start experiencing this joy of freedom from the mind and start becoming centered in the self the more you would be driven, enthusiastic to make this freedom permanent.

Your outer world is simply a reflection of the state of your mind. Positive mindset people have a very positive world out there for them, positive people, positive situations/events, they are able to see positivity in everything around them. Negative mindset people have a very negative world out there for them, negative people and negative situations/events. And the ultimate free person transcends both the positive and negative and is stable and centered and in bliss forever.

Bliss is not an emotion. Bliss is the ultimate state of your being. In this state you are not shaken and moved by anything instead you are simply in a state of witness, centered in your self. That self which is your true nature and not the ego based "I." It is this self which is connected to the source/ the divine whereas the mind is which is bound to the body and it is actions.

The self is always guided by the source and what is guided by the highest is never categorized into anything dual like good or bad, happy or sad, right or wrong. Duality is of the mind. Judgement is of the mind. Analysis is of the mind. Impressions are of the mind. Self is ever free and not entangled by anything. It is just like a pure white canvas. So, if you are guided by the self to do anything and even if your mind muddles in and categorizes it into good or bad, right or wrong, simply go ahead and do as per the guidance of the self.

Just imagine how any entanglement feels like and looks like. It is suffocating and stifling. It creates boundaries and keeps you stuck. This is what exactly mind does. It entangles you in attachments, emotions, feelings and reactions. People and events do not hurt you. It is your own mind which brings you the pain because it keeps you stuck and entangled in people and events. Self-mastery is breaking free from this entanglement. When you are stable in your self, in your soul then you are never entangled in any person, event, emotion, feeling or thought.

The ultimate purpose of this journey is the evolution of your soul to reach the higher dimensions and ultimately be self-realized. There are no "should do," "supposed to do" in this path. Self has no pattern. It can guide you to be the CEO of a big organization or guide you to start farming and drop everything else. Mind creates images of what spirituality should be like and what worldly life is supposed to be. This duality is created by the mind. All segregations are of the mind.

The golden rule of self-realization is that there is no rule book, no method. It happens randomly and rarely also. The image of a spiritual way of living from time immemorial has been that of leaving everything and running away to the mountains and the monasteries. On the other hand, the image of a worldly life has been that of luxury and goods and comfort. Both are illusionary images of the mind.

When you are guided by your soul there is no concept to follow. It can guide you to be an entrepreneur or guide you to be a farmer. Nothing is right and nothing is wrong. Simply listen to the voice of the heart - your soul. You can be both externally rich and internally peaceful at the same time only if you learn how not to get attached to anything fleeting. Money in itself is not bad it is your relationship with it that is the deal breaker.

Spirituality is not an act or just a set of practices. Spirituality is not about becoming someone special, or different. Spirituality is when one accepts life as it is, when one accepts the present moment. It is the way of your true being. One who is truly spiritual understands this fact that there will be suffering and happiness both. A spiritual person will not take events of life as a surprise, as they understand this is life and suffering and happiness both shall pass soon. Now death also cannot shake them because they understand that death is natural, it will happen to everybody.

Only when you stop listening to other people's opinions and choices would you ever be able to listen to the voice of your soul. Self never competes, self never follows. Self just is. Only when you know your self would you ever know anything about this existence.

May 19th, 2023

Bengaluru, India

19. Simplicity is Divinity

There are so many things that one needs to work on oneself in order to become a good human being. In the garb of spirituality, we cannot hide ourselves. Things that need to be worked upon should be worked upon. Build loving, caring and honest relationships with your family members, your siblings, your friends, your colleagues at work. Without love and compassion for everyone do not even call yourself a human. It must be genuine and unconditional love. Go into every relationship to give and not to get. Do not get into any relationship to fill your vacuum. This vacuum needs to be filled by yourself by going deep within through meditation and other spiritual practices.

Go ahead and apologize to your family members or your friends if you have hurt them. Go and hug them like there will not be a next time. Do not be stubborn that you are always right. Own your mistakes. Apologize first always and then learn and move on. Work on your patience, your greed, your anger, your jealousy. Be patient with everyone in your life. Forgive everyone. Do not be so self-consumed.

Work on your rigidness and superficiality. Do not be judgmental. Be free spirited and non-judgmental the way you were when you were a child. Be simple. Do not try to show-off. True spirituality is simplicity. Genuine peace and happiness can only be found in simplicity. Those who are truly wise are simple. Be humble and thankful for all your blessings in your life. Simplify your life, live in the present, share positive things with people and let the meditation happen and silence prevail.

Do not build spiritual ego and get hardened and judgmental because of it. Do not fool yourself under the pretext of spirituality by labelling yourself as 'being spiritual.' Wearing this spiritual badge of honour is just like adding another label the way you have done with your name and position. 'Being Spiritual' certainly implies that others are ignorant and you are the knower, others are unspiritual and you are spiritual. This is subtle ego in action known as spiritual ego. This is once again the duality created by the conditioned mind. Be aware of falling in this trap.

Love your parents, your whole family for the unconditional love and support that they have all always given and continue to give you. Be kind and generous to everyone, daily, every minute. True spirituality is more about becoming a good human being first before anything else. It is about getting rid of all your shadow sides. Learn to accept people and situations/events as they are. Do not try to change anyone instead show them the light. Share what path and practices you followed that brought huge transformations in your life. Share how you remain happy during difficult periods of life. You have the treasure, but if somebody is not interested in taking it, can you give it? No. Like Buddha said- "Appo Deepo Bhava" (Be your own light). It means that everyone is alone and responsible for their own changes and growth. So, you can just show them the path and tell them the ways, but the actual walk is to be taken by them.

Do not always react to everything instead take a pause and then respond. Always be soft in your speech be it verbal or written. Your words and actions should always heal others and not harm others. Maintain peaceful and harmonious relationships with everyone. Do not be so possessive that you have to be the number one priority in everyone's life. Give people the freedom to choose. Wait patiently for their love towards you. Do not demand but instead give. Give and offer your love to people. Awaken the divinity in everyone through your speech, actions and presence.

August 21ˢᵗ, 2023

Bengaluru, India

20. The Purpose of Life

Between a good thought and a bad thought always choose the good thought. Make it a conscious effort and a discipline to pick only good and positive thoughts throughout the day. Make it a practice till it engrains into a habit. Actions cannot get completed if all your thoughts are negative about yourself, about your abilities. Negative thoughts weaken your body, mind and soul.

Always affirm that you are a powerful soul. Put affirmations that strengthen your soul and not the affirmations that strengthen your mind. Putting positive affirmations to get a good job, career, success, relationships, health etc. is simply strengthening the mind. Ask and pray for the highest and the highest is knowing your true self only.

Life can be very dull and meaningless if you are not working on your soul purpose. True happiness and "life" come to your being when you find your purpose and start working on it. Self-mastery is the journey of finding your true authentic self and doing what your soul's purpose is.

Till you find your soul purpose you are simply running around in circles in the quest of happiness.

Every activity that we do in our life is simply our quest for happiness and love. But that true happiness and love is revealed when you start walking on the path of your soul purpose. All other happiness will always be transient in nature. Your soul's purpose could be just about anything. It might not necessarily be about changing the world or doing anything that is very grand or comes with name and fame. You soul's purpose could simply be gardening, painting, writing, creating art etc.

It is for you to introspect and find your soul's purpose. No other person on this planet can ever tell you what your soul purpose is. If someone does tell you that then please run as far as possible from them. Take guidance but always listen to your own divine voice from within. Your soul's purpose would be revealed only when you have strengthened your inner voice enough for you to follow it.

Life has no limitations set by age, gender, society, religion or caste. You can start doing anything at any age, at any place, at any point in time in your life. Life is not just about surviving. Life is about thriving. You can learn dancing at the age of 50, you can write a book at the age of 80. Limitations are always of the mind. It creates barriers. But if you are truly free then you can do anything. The mind accumulates, the body deteriorates but the soul is ever free ready to thrive in the present moment. Whatever you truly like to do or is your true passion you would never need any push for it. Try to seek that passion from within.

However, sometimes motivation is required by people to sit in meditation and that is purely because they understand that meditation would help them in silencing their mind and shedding its layers to reveal the true self. Meditation is just a means and not the end.

Once you are self-realized then no motivation is needed as every single step of your life is guided by the self. So here knowledge should not be misunderstood that if someone guides you or motivates you to sit in mediation so that you can connect to your true self then you should not listen to them. One should follow the advice as it is the starting point. Sitting in meditation, sitting in silence are the starting points towards your discovery of the self, your true nature.

21. Fall to Rise Up

You cannot rise up till you have hit rock bottom. Hitting rock bottom is a golden gateway towards total transformation. You might never do any self-introspection or self-analysis till you have hit rock bottom. This is the only place perhaps where transformation actually takes birth. Transformation can never happen on the surface level of life that most people live at. This golden opportunity will burn you down into ashes so that you can rise up like a phoenix. Nothing moves without energy. You might own a Ferrari but if there is no fuel in it then it is as good as being a piece of scrap. Similarly, you yourself are like a Ferrari but with no energy you cannot function at all.

The higher the energy the higher the bliss, the higher you are able to function. Life is a constant flow. The moment you are stuck, you are dead with no energy. The only fuel that life needs is your consistent high energy. The more the external factors are the source of your energy the more depleted your life and enthusiasm would be. The day the very fact that you have come alone in this life and would go back alone is engrained in your consciousness that day you are set on the path to the ultimate freedom.

Just a superficial intellectual understanding of this knowledge, this wisdom is not enough for you to feel it that way. You need to experience it; you need to live it and that can only happen in solitude and spending days just by yourself till you start enjoying your own company thoroughly and totally.

You are valuable already. In fact, priceless. Do not try to increase your value by associating yourself with objects that your conditioned mind and ego considers as valuable.

December 7ᵗʰ, 2023

New Delhi, India

22. Sincere Seeking

Journey to the self is a very bold and courageous journey. It is not for the weak. It is a conscious choice that you will have to make if you are going to dedicate this lifetime of yours in seeking your true authentic self or living a life run by your conditioned mind - false ego. Intuition is something that is beyond your logical mind. Silencing your mind is the way to improve your intuition.

Meditation is the only way to silence your mind. It is a conscious choice that you will have to make if you want to take out some time in the day to do your daily spiritual practices, your mediation or let the whole day pass in doing the daily mundane stuff that you have been doing for years together.

I believe this is the only free will one has to be able to choose what one wants to do in that moment. A lot of people get scared and fearful when they go through some sort of existential crisis and give up the hope on life itself. In fact, existential crisis is a boon if you ever come face to face with it. This crisis is an opportunity for you to experience and understand the shallowness of life itself when it is lived at the surface level of eating, sleeping, running after money, careers, status, relationships etc. This crisis forces you to look deep within and take a journey towards finding out who you truly are beyond this body and mind, emotions and feelings.

Journey to the self is like going through fire. In this process be prepared to get your ego crushed, your emotions and feelings thrashed. True self is hidden behind the mask of the false ego - mind. You raise a new born child with tribal people and he would become like them. You raise the same new born child in the richest house of the world and his mind would get conditioned accordingly. Your mind can be conditioned, can be changed and hence it is not the truth.

Anything that changes is not the truth. Your true self - your soul is the only truth. You have been born only and only to realize this truth but the world conditions you so badly and so deeply that you simply forget who you truly are. The difference between your soul and the mind can be realized only through meditation and being in a state of awareness – witness consciousness.

For most people the soul has become completely silent and weak since it has never been listened to. It is the mind which is running the show for most of them. And whenever it is the mind running the show, the show will never end no matter how happy or sorrowful it is. And you will keep on taking birth after birth. Focus on getting free, on getting liberated and not just about getting happy all the time. Happiness and sadness will always come and go just like waves in the ocean. Focus on becoming the ocean. Freedom is the ultimate bliss millions of miles ahead of the most happy moment that can ever be experienced.

Happiness and sadness are two sides of the same coin. Whenever you are happy, be ready to be sad. Sadness is a shadow of happiness. Happiness and sadness both are stressed states of mind. The happiness which looks like an ocean eventually turns out to be the desert of sand. Happiness and sadness are outside, but silence comes from inside. Seek silence, not happiness.

December 12th, 2023

New Delhi, India

23. Reality vs Illusion

What appears is not the true reality always. Let me share this through a true analogy that happened with me and how my awareness just observed it and brought about this beautiful insight. I have a particular font of text on my laptop screen and then I switched to a different laptop which had a much smaller font as compared to my original laptop screen. I worked on this other screen which had a much smaller font for a long time and when I switched back to my original laptop the font on it appeared to be much larger than it actually was. This happened simply because my eyes got accustomed to seeing something different for a prolonged time and this completely altered my vision.

What I am meaning to say here is that just because you have lived an illusion for a long time it is bound to alter your view of the reality as well. But the truth never changes, it is our vision that gets altered. Consciousness is teaching and showing us signs all the time but it is on us if we are aware enough to recognize these signs. Mind always operates from a place of lack. If not this then that.

It always needs to latch on to something for it is survival as its breeding ground. No matter what emotion or feeling arises in you be it of being happy or sad, being angry or elated, being guilty or proud etc. if you are simply able to witness the emotion or feeling arising in you then it holds no power over you.

Witnessing simply dissolves it. And this becomes your step-by-step journey in conquering the mind. Nothing remains permanent in this world that is why we call it as an illusion. What is there now will be gone tomorrow. That is the nature of this world. The biggest illusion that everyone lives in is the individual world created by their mind which they consider as reality. Your deemed reality is the creation of your individual mind.

In Bhagavad Gita Arjuna tells Lord Krishna that "The mind is very restless, turbulent, strong and obstinate, O Krishna. It appears to me that it is more difficult to control than the wind." Alas! nothing can be truer than this. Lord Krishna replied to Arjuna saying that "For him who has conquered the mind, the mind is the best of friends; but for one who has failed to do so, his very mind will be the greatest enemy."

Positive thoughts, positive emotions and positive feelings and your deemed reality, the world that you have created for yourself appears to be positive. Negative thoughts, negative emotions and negative feelings and your whole world appears to be negative. If you can become a witness to everything in every moment then you are free, you are liberated. Nothing can move you; nothing can shake you. But since we fail to witness what is happening within us most of the times, we start reacting to everything and everyone. When you witness you respond. When you do not witness you react.

The world will bake you; the world will shake you but if you remain steadfast in your determination to be free you have simply made it. Bravo! Many times, people and situations/events would become so rough for you that your own mind will pounce on every such opportunity to de-rail your journey. But remember the journey to self is not the journey of being happy but instead it is the journey of being free. If you want to be happy or sad then stay in your mind. But if you want eternal freedom then get to know your true self. The self that has been coated over by millions of lifetimes of conditionings and impressions.

Remember you soul has taken many forms so it carries forward all those past tendencies or impressions whenever you take birth. And then you put another coat of the conditionings and behavioral patterns of the present lifetime as well over it. There is a lot to uncover and too less a time. Sometimes it takes lifetimes to reach your true self. This a journey of the warriors and not the weaker ones. You have been asleep for lifetimes and if you continue to be asleep in this one as well then no one can really help you. A lot of times it may seem that you are lost but remember only those who lose themselves will ever find themselves. Only when you knock at all the wrong doors will you ever find the right one for you.

There would be times when you will have no plan whatsoever for the near future or the distant future because the mind has taken a backset now. There is an unabashed, unapologetic sense of freeness you will feel. Remember it is the mind only that plans. Self is ever spontaneous and in the present moment. It is the mind which does all the planning and brings with it all the fears, insecurities, anxieties and worries of the future which has not even come.

The one who has the tendency to live life through the mind will fall apart in such circumstances as there are no plans for the future.

The one who lives consciously and with awareness lives only in the present moment as it is the only truth that exists. Fear and worry stop you from living life fully and becoming the authentic you. It is what stops you from unleashing the infinite potential that is within you. The opposite of fear is not fearlessness. Opposite of fear is courage. Courage is about moving into the unknown despite having fear and uncertainty. Courage is about saying "Yes" and taking responsibility for the consequences. Courage is also about saying "No" and being ready for the consequences. Courage means living life by heart. Life is beautiful, no matter what happens.

You are the universe, you are the creator, you are the divine. It is the ego mind that has given you a separate identity. Your identification with the different labels that you carry has become so firm that you have forgotten who you truly are.

Take action for the things that need to be done but do not be feverish about its results. Leaving all feverishness for the results, desires, wants is a stepping stone in your journey back home. Your soul has taken birth in your present body to come back to the source and be where it truly belongs. It has not taken this birth to become what your conditioned mind wants it to become. If there is one gift in this whole world that you can ever give yourself then gift yourself the present moment. Gift yourself the awareness to be always steadfast in the present moment and not to oscillate between the past and the future.

There is no two ever. But because of the false ego you identify yourself as a separate identity from the universe. It is the same consciousness, universe, god, cosmos, awareness – different names for the same truth that has appeared in different shapes and forms. You are simply one of it is forms. The person you love the most is the same consciousness, the same universe presenting itself in the form of your loved one. Similarly, the person you dislike the most is also the same consciousness, the same universe presenting itself in the form of this person. You also are the same universe. There is only one and not two.

Then what is there to hate and what is there to love. It is all ONE. You already are Sat-Chit-Anand. You do not have to attain it. You simply have to uncover it for the truth to reveal on it is own. It cannot be found. It cannot be searched. It is already there. You simply have to realize it and be eternally free and that is what is known as self-realization and self-actualization.

In this journey to uncover the truth learn to set healthy boundaries from the ones who have the capacity to pull you towards the world run by the mind. Be alert and conscious that if the company you keep is making you operate more from the mind or more from the heart. Choose the company of the latter always. This journey is truly the journey of moving down from the head to the heart. The more you will live your life from the heart the closer you get to the real self.

Your heart is the bridge between materialistic life and spiritual life. Trust, love, gratitude, compassion and surrender are the signs of a person who lives from his heart. Heart is the seat of the soul. Living by heart means living close to the soul and when you live close to the soul, the insights will generate within you. These insights are directly from the soul. Insights are the wisdom of the soul. One who aspires a spiritual journey, insights help, insights guide, and insights help you to expand your consciousness. You can listen, talk to your consciousness when you are living by the heart, without that the false ego mind has an endless distance from the soul.

Anybody can learn to listen to their heart. The path to your soul goes through the heart. God is not somewhere in the sky - his home is in your heart. All noise belongs to the mind (ego) and whatsoever humans know as love, prayer and meditation belong to the heart. Love, prayer and meditation are synonymous because you get the taste of them in the state of egolessness. Your heart beats in this very moment and if you start to live 'here and now' slowly you will start listening to your heart.

Many times, when you are operating in the world doing all the worldly activities there will be a great tendency to get completely lost and get entangled in such activities and lose complete sense of awareness and the present moment. In all such moments physically tap your body and speak "here and now," "here and now" and bring your awareness to the present moment.

When you do your daily routine tasks, practice mindfulness. Mindfulness means timelessness. Have you ever observed that when you do your favourite activity you lose track of time? Being available to "here and now" is mindfulness. When you work you should be mindful and with that it means one should be totally engrossed into what one is doing – "here and now." You will observe it makes you much more efficient and meditative too. It makes any task a play and any work a piece of art. This is one part of meditation.

The other part is witnessing. One should simply keep one hour each day for themselves. Go to nature and walk into the nature. Find a place to sit and close your eyes and just listen to the sounds around you and feel the cool breeze on your face, all inclusive. Nothing to choose! This way you can live a life of meditation.

It is same consciousness that is playing a game in different shapes and forms. The form through which it wants to experience self-realization it will experience it through that. The form through which it wants to experience materialism – the world it will experience it through that. If you are the chosen one to be awakened then in the form of your body the universe will experience awakening. If the universe wants to experience materialism through others, then nothing in this world can awaken them or bring them on the spiritual path. So never judge anyone or anything. It is simply not a part of their syllabus for this lifetime. Universe wants to experience different things through them so there is no need to judge anyone's journey of life whatsoever. Everything is determined by Karma. Karma of previous lifetimes and karma of this lifetime too.

Every person or situation/event that you encounter in your journey of self-mastery is the universe showing you a mirror for what needs to be fixed within you so that you can move forward and uncover your true authentic self. Never take a person or situation/event personally. It is you only - the universe in a different shape and form triggering you to get rid of your patterns and your mental conditionings. These people and situations/events that you encounter are simply your test papers. Until you learn what is to be learnt through them, they will keep on coming again and again lifetime after lifetime till the time the lesson is learnt fully and karma with them is dissolved completely. And you do not want to fail in this exam. Do You?

Sometimes the universe will send people who are in the same journey to soften or ease it a bit for you and sometimes you will be left in the cold. Be prepared for anything and everything. The journey to the summit can either take multiple births or just an instant. That is dependent on total grace. But you keep on marching onwards and upwards.

December 20th, 2023

New Delhi, India

24. Self vs Ego

People generally talk about living life fully. But no one teaches you to how to do that. A wholesome and fulfilled life can be lived only through intuition and inner soul guidance. Engage as much as possible with individuals who live their lives through their hearts, their soul's wisdom and are not dictated by the tyrant mind.

Guilt consciousness is the biggest obstacle in your journey to self-mastery. Do not ever feel guilty of what you have been like in the past. What truly matters is what you do now. Are you making a choice to live consciously or un-consciously. Every action where you are in awareness/witness consciousness becomes a conscious action and every action where you are not in the witness consciousness becomes an unconscious action.

The biggest challenges you would encounter in this journey would come from the people and the situations/events where the shackles of attachment and your identification with them is the highest. It is not a selfish journey contrary to what your mind would contest now and would like you to believe. In fact, it is a journey of becoming selfless. Every defeat of the mind is the victory of the soul. And the more the choices made by your soul win the stronger the soul becomes.

Like Ramana Maharshi (an enlightened master) said - "The only useful purpose of the present birth is to turn within and realize the Self. There is nothing else to do." Every single time you have taken body you have played the same game but under different names, labels and identities. The one who has become bored of this game or has been awakened to the futility of it will automatically walk towards the path of self-realization.

Boredom is a gift. The more you connect with your soul the more you will realize that it is a god damn play run by the mind and the mind wants to play this game through the body in an endless loop. Till the time you are self-realized it will be a constant battle between the mind and the heart. Many times, you would experience that even though you are making a conscious choice to live by the heart/soul the old conditions, the old patterns of the mind still come to the surface. You would be living moment by moment and feeling content with what you have and suddenly you will meet someone who would start talking about an achievement-based life, what success should be like and things one should be doing so that the ego is satisfied.

Ego is the layer that separates you from others. And all the endeavors of ego-based life are to prove to the "other."

The "other" who does not even exist but for your ego to be satiated the other must be there. You might feel lost in such situations that if you should fall back to the egoistical mind or continue listening to your soul? This will create a lot of push and pull and people will constantly remind you of your old self. They cannot relate to the "new" you and their preconceived notions label you as "you are so lost."

Every time your ego breaks it creates a lot of negativity or let us call it suffering around you. You might lose your job, your house, your relationships, your health be it anything that the ego identifies with. The moment that happens fear, suffering and pain surfaces in your life. Ego has no more to identify with. What is there to show off to others. What is there to prove? What is there to accumulate? But remember fear is also a blessing because those who can conquer their fears and defeat their ego win life. The root of your suffering is your ignorance of your true nature, your true self.

The death of your ego is the real death. What is there when your physical body dies. That is not even death. The one who has experienced the death of ego is the one who has truly lived their life. When you die, your body dies. When your ego dies then the whole world and its attachments die. Journey to the self means taking out the beads of desires and attachments one by one from the garland of worldly life. When you realize the futility of everything that is when you take a step towards infinity.

The conditioning of each mind is different because of past memories, past experiences, previous lifetimes, previous karmas and the current actions. Whatever are the experiences of the minds of different people the same thing they want to impose on you also. And that is how societies and clans are formed. A group of people having similar mindset will form one society, one set of belief-systems and so on and so forth. All these societal constructs are made by people and broken by people because minds change and the new set of minds then make new rules and new societal constructs.

But when you are self -realized and awakened then the universe, nature, god, divine, higher soul, awareness, cosmos, consciousness whatever you may want to refer it as takes over and whatever needs to be done is done through you. You are no longer the doer. Whatever is the will of the universe passes through you. You are free forever and ever. And you want to bargain this freedom for the golden cage that mind creates life after life for you?

This journey of the self is not about anything external but about becoming complete within itself. It can be an enduring or a non-enduring journey. All depends on your courage. There has never been and never will be a rule book for self-realization. It is unique and original for every single person. There is no formula or an eligibility criterion that needs to be met. You can definitely read about the experiences of each such individual who has been self-realized. But would it guarantee self-realization, not a chance.

Just be natural always and start living from your heart and your journey has begun. You will have to fight a lot of battles along the way. And these battles are simply the thoughts, emotions and feelings that emanate from your mind. The more ego-centric, the more mind-oriented you will be the tougher the battles, the tougher the challenges would be. You mind, your ego-based attachments, labels, identifications do not die so quickly. You have fed them and nourished them for many lifetimes. You were taught all your life to become successful and have achievement-based goals, follow the trends and careers that reap you the maximum money and status. The ego, the mind never gave you an opportunity to find out and realize what is that you are actually good at.

However, one beautiful transformation that you will experience in this journey is that as your mind conditioning dies your natural talents come to the surface. Talents that you never knew existed within you. You will start doing activities which give you true joy and peace without even looking for any material benefit out of it. But be rest assured nature always rewards us when anything is done from the heart.

Each one of us is endowed with creativity but if it is not recognized and nurtured by you then it will never blossom in your life. Each time you create something new you expand your consciousness and the same thing happens when you meditate. Creativity and meditation go together. If you are unable to sit and meditate then dance and music are meditation for you.

Whatever comes from the soul always reaches the soul. Have you ever observed that? One needs to be sensitive enough to realize this phenomenon. Some people have become so hardened by their mind constructs that even a soulful thing takes a U-turn from their mind and fails to touch their soul. It never penetrates their heart. Any soulful act is simply considered meaningless by them.

Here being sensitive does not mean being weak or emotional but being sensitive means one whose soul is more powerful than their mind. Always chose your soul's guidance over the formalities, societal constructs and social obligations no matter how strongly the mind identifies with these labels and attachments.

The smile that comes from ego-mind based acts stands pale in front of the smile that comes after doing a soulful act. The only connection that you need is with your self and all your external connections are taken care of. When your mind drops the illusionary world drops. When the soul shines the reality shines. Let the world call you crazy, stupid, selfish, eccentric, lost etc. and you can add to the list. Do not fret. The minds of the world cannot survive without giving labels and identities to anything and everything or else they find it next to impossible to relate to it. It is the job of the mind to compare and relate.

Do not ever blame them because they themselves truly do not know what they are doing and why they are doing it.

Keep witnessing, keep moving forward. You already are everything that you are seeking outside of you. You just need to uncover this truth. The goldmine, the treasure of love, happiness, joy, peace is already within you and you unknowingly are seeking all of it through your relationships, careers, money, statuses, labels outside in the hope that all these transient and temporary things would give you the eternal happiness.

The cup has a form but what is useful is the empty space inside the cup. It is the empty space that holds the water. And realizing that empty space within is truly coming back home. Day and night the one who is asleep and unaware of his true authentic self is fighting tooth and nail lifetime after lifetime to achieve, accomplish and accumulate the temporary things that are capable of giving small joys only. He is completely ignorant to the taste of the never-ending nectar available within. He has bartered the elixir of freedom with these temporary joys of life. How ignorant? How foolish?

April 27th, 2024

Bengaluru, India

25. What is Love

Love is the most mis-understood world especially in the modern world that we belong to. Have you ever thought what is true love? What is the reality of true love? Love happens at three levels. The first and the lowest manifestation of love is based on the ego/mind. It is the level where the other is needed and where one is engrossed in sexuality. With this type of love the physical form is a must. One cannot imagine love without the physical form. At this level "I' is very important and this "I" is deeply rooted. Here one desires for something and expects the other to fulfill. Here love has to become pain and suffering someday as it is dependent on somebody. Such a love where mind is always ahead, chaos is great.

The second manifestation of love happens where heart is ahead of the mind and the love has blossomed to the heart. Here the "I" starts dissolving and the physical form is not needed anymore as love is deep within. Here the mind is little more evolved and starts believing in some particular form of god as per the belief of their culture or family tradition. This type of love is termed as devotion and devotion takes you beyond your body and mind into the heart.

The third and the highest manifestation is where love has turned into greatest compassion. Here no person or no particular god is needed as love itself has become your state of mind. This love takes you beyond the body, mind and the god. Here one carries compassion for everyone. There is no enemy or friend. Everyone gets the love. Here lover and love are not two. There is no greater power in this world than the power of this love. Trust, forgiveness, gratitude and surrender are pillars of this love. This love can melt anything.

26. Surrender to the Eternal

Do a complete surrender to your inner self. Do not get influenced by people, places or situations/events. Make choices that resonate with your heart even if they puzzle others. Memories are something that are already dead but mind lingers onto the memories whether they are good or bad. But life is here and now, past and the future are in your mind. When you start to live in the now then your wounds disappear automatically. One quick tip to be happy is to have new insights every day. This is how your consciousness expands on a daily basis. Step into the fire of self-mastery, self-discovery. This fire will not burn you; it will only burn what you are not.

Nothing outside of you has power over you. Do not always try to fix whoever or whatever comes in your life. Find out your true authentic self so that no matter what comes or goes you are always centered. If you resonate with all this that means you are being prepared for something incredible. Be grateful and be ready. Ignoring your intuition and denying what your heart resonates with is self-betrayal. Do not ever allow the illusion of "boredom" or "loneliness" make you return to patterns, behaviors, habits, people and situations that you no longer want to experience.

Boredom or loneliness are precious gaps or pauses, opportunities for reflection, growth and self-discovery. Mind is what makes you think who you should be. Self is who you are. The more fearful you are the more you are run by your mind. The more fearless you are the more you are run by your heart. Once you start loving yourself everything would flow to you naturally.

Mind is so used to activity that it panics whenever there is no activity. Silence of mind is the death of the mind. If you sit idle doing nothing and simply practice witnessing all thoughts and emotions and take no action on them initially the mind would create a lot of panic and a lot of fear that you are not doing anything. When you do nothing, just sit and watch - nothing remains unsettled forever. This is not in the nature of existence to remain unsettled. The existence keeps moving from order to disorder and disorder to order. Your life too moves from order to disorder and disorder to order. Turmoil is bound to settle.

You are angry, just sit and do nothing - anger is bound to settle. There is an irrefutable law of nature working underneath. Buddha's enlightenment (or every enlightenment) happened because when there was nothing to do, neither outward nor inward he became available to now and here. Enlightenment is the fruit of effortlessness - non-doing. Every technique, every method you come across is to get bored of it and move on to the next till your mind gives up and becomes "shoonya -nothingness"

Your path is more difficult because your calling is higher. Make it happen. Only you can do that. Fall in love with this journey of becoming your true authentic self. Have the fierce courage to break the old patterns that are no longer serving you and believe me you can do that.

The nature of the mind is to run after fulfilling compulsive desires which eventually takes you into an infinite loop of desire and wish fulfillment. People become so driven by such unconscious needs and desires to validate their existence in the society, in the world that they sacrifice their playfulness and joyfulness in return.

But when you witness a compulsive desire arising in you and take no action on it then the mind's tendency of wanting to fulfill all such compulsive desires gradually fades away. For example, you get a compulsive desire to buy the next new gadget that has come in the market which you do not even need, simply watch it and take no action on it. Mind is like a child who has been playing outside for way too long. Break this habit and form a new habit of taking the mind inwards till the time comes when the mind dissolves completely into the self and only the self remains.

The crux of an authentic life or authentic spirituality is the quest to know one's ownself. A sure way to progress on this journey is to remain detached even while leading an active material life in the world. True detachment is to live without duality - likes and dislikes (e.g. love and hate, friend and enemy, joy and sorrow etc.). As long as a person believes in love for some and hate for others (i.e. likes and dislikes), his union with self/soul/divine/god remains difficult.

You are the Light. You are the Creator. You are the Divine. You already are whatever you are seeking. Love and embrace your "inner self" so much till you realize you already are that love that you have always been seeking outside of you through various relationships and material possessions. You can never love the "other." Love can never exist as long as there is two, as long as there is duality. It is only attachment that you have towards the "other" that you have been calling as love. Only when you become love can you even offer love. And this love flows towards everyone, towards all creations of the world, towards the entire existence. As long as your love is for "someone" and not "everyone" be rest assured it is just an outcome of your previous karma with that person(s), an outcome of your desire, lust, greed and want.

This has been my experience so far and I hope it sheds some light on your path. Let this journey continue till "you" and "me" meet again, the "duality" ends and only "oneness" remains.

Afterword

Truth is within us. Start your journey. It will change your life. Knowledge is that which liberates. It should liberate you from all those defilements, all those barriers that block you from knowing yourself. Knowing the infinite within you is the aim of life. The privilege of human lifetime is to search oneself and know oneself to become who you truly are.

Help yourself realize the life's ultimate purpose. We can get any worldly work done by any other person, but we have to do the work of self-improvement ourselves. True spirituality is of the SELF, for the SELF, by the SELF. No one else can help you in crossing over. It is a personal journey that requires self-efforts. When effort is coupled with surrender, the effort becomes "effortless effort." Truth is not outside – it is within. If Truth was outside of us, then one could go in a group, in the company of people. But since the truth is not outside of us but within us, we cannot go there in a company or a group. Thus, the path has to be traveled alone. If we do not arrive "home" within "here and now," then there is nobody to blame!

If a wave can know or find itself, then it will realize that it is not separate from the ocean!

If a ray can know or find itself, then it will realize that it is not separate from the sun!

If an ornament can know or find itself, then it will realize that it is not separate from the gold!

If an earthen pot can know or find itself, then it will realize that it is not separate from the clay!

This only is Self-realization - to know one's essential nature as Pure Awareness.

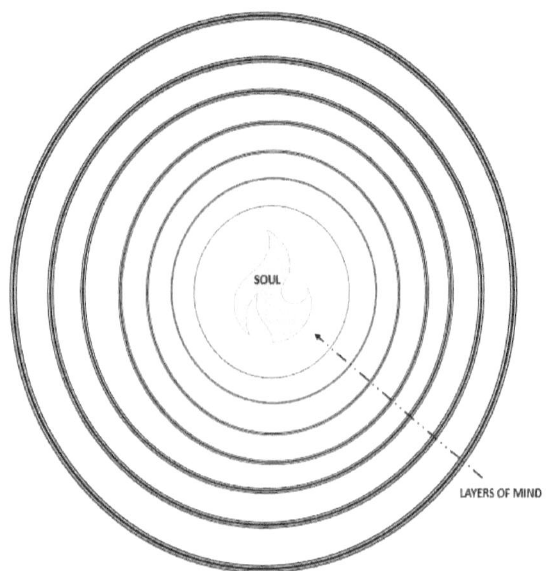